World's Best
MOTORCYCLES

INSIDE THE ACCLAIMED MC COLLECTION OF STOCKHOLM

Guy Fithen &
Christer R. Christensson

Published by:
Wilkinson Publishing Pty Ltd
ACN 006 042 173
Level 4, 2 Collins St Melbourne, Victoria, Australia 3000
Ph: +61 3 9654 5446
www.wilkinsonpublishing.com

International distribution by Pineapple Media Limited
(www.pineapple-media.com)   ISSN 2200 – 9882

National Library of Australia Cataloguing-in-Publication entry
Creator: Fithen, Guy, author.
Title: World's best motorcycles /
            Guy Fithen & Christer R Christensson.
ISBN: 9781925265569 (paperback)
Subjects: Motorcycles--History--Pictorial works.
            Motorcycles--Design and construction.
Other Creators/Contributors:
            Christensson, Christer R., author.
Dewey Number: 629.2275

Photos by Ola Österling from the MC Collection Stockholm
and agreement with GettyImages.

Design: Michael Bannenberg
Printed in China.

Contents

THE MC COLLECTION   vi

Henderson 1912   1

Indian Board Track Racer 1913   8

Flying Merkel 1914   16

Brough SS100 1925   22

Harley-Davidson Peashooter 1926   30

Husqvarna 500 cc Single 1931   38

Crocker Big tank 1939   46

Vincent C Rapide c 1951   54

BMW Rennsport RS54 1954   62

MV Agusta Monoalbero Corsa 1954   70

AJS 7R Racer 1960   78

Matchless G50 1962   86

Lito X Cam 1967   94

Honda CR750 1971   102

Rob North Triumph Trident 750cc 1975   110

Harley-Davidson XR1000 1983   118

MV Agusta F4 Serie d'Oro 2000   126

Vyrus 984 C3 2V 2007   134

BMW HP2 Sport 2010   142

m⊃⊂ollection

The MC Collection represents over 50 years of private collecting by Christer R Christensson, and the work of his colleague, Ove Johansson, and his highly-skilled team of restorers, to bring together an extensive catalogue of the very best of motorcycle design and technology.

The MC Collection is intended to present the motorcycle as mechanical sculpture and honour all motorcycle design engineers from the very first motorcycle produced, the Hilderbrand & Wolfmueller of 1894, to the state-of-the-art machines of today.

In 1999, Christer R Christensson took the decision to re-house his unique personal collection in a purpose-built showroom at Sollentuna, near Stockholm, Sweden, and open it to the public to enable wider audiences to enjoy some of the most rare and desirable motorcycles in the world.

This publication showcases a small selection of just some of the 400 extraordinary machines that make up the MC Collection. Together, they provide a unique viewpoint on the history of technical innovation and progress in two-wheeled design.

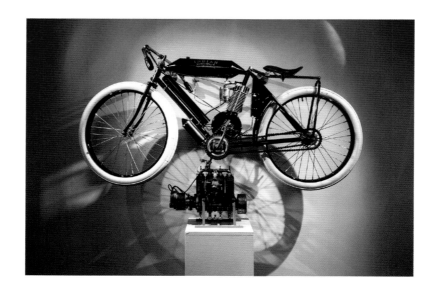

The MC Collection is a
"museum of art, a museum that
exhibits mechanical sculptures."

Henderson 1912 USA

Engine:	Inlet over exhaust in-line 4 cyl
Frame:	Tubular steel cradle
Suspension:	Leading axle
Weight:	295 lbs / 134 kg
Capacity:	56cu / 920cc
Power:	8hp / 6kw
Top Speed:	60mph / 100kph

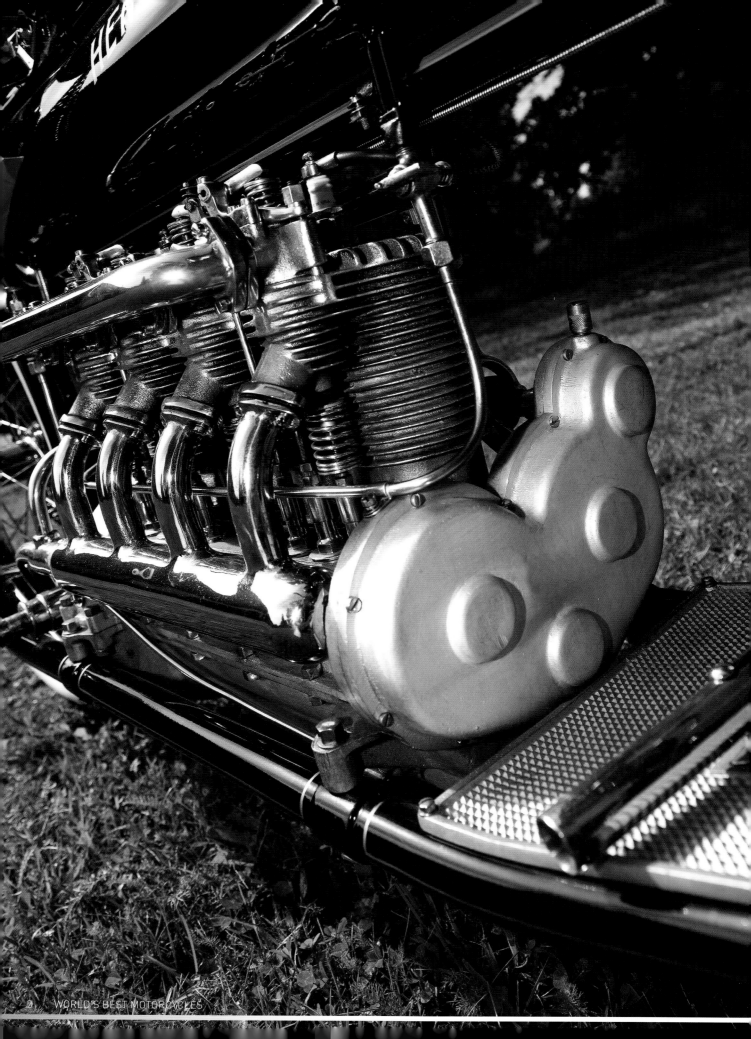

Motorcyclists retain a vivid memory of the first time they rode a four cylinder machine. The smooth delivery of power is so unlike the thump of single or twin cylinders, and the howl from the exhausts of a 'four' under hard acceleration is not easily forgotten.

In the years before the Great War, the Henderson four cylinder was renowned as the epitome of refined motorcycling. Everything about the brand stood for quality and elegance, painstakingly designed by William Henderson to be 'the finest motorcycle in the world'.

William set out to make the Henderson bigger, faster, better, than the competition, and with his brother, Thomas, running their family business in Detroit, intended to conquer the motorcycle world. It was perhaps unsurprising that of all the designs that William put forward for consideration to his father, a vice president of the Winton Motor Car Company, it was a four cylinder design that eventually passed scrutiny.

The Henderson was by no means the only four cylinder motorcycle on offer in the early years of motorcycling. Paul Kelecom had designed a revolutionary shaft-driven four cylinder model for the Belgium company FN that went into production as early as 1903 and a number of American factories were to build four-cylinder machines, including first Pierce, in 1909, and later Cleveland, Indian and Excelsior.

The Henderson positioned the engine low and in-line with the frame which inevitably gave it a long wheelbase. This made it stable at speed and also meant there was plenty of room for an optional seat for a passenger, in this case not behind the rider, tandem-style, but in front, as though on a bicycle cross-bar. While not ideal for the rider's view of the road ahead, one advantage of this arrangement is that the long, pull-back handlebars gave the rider plenty of leverage to help keep everything straight and under control on the rough roads of the time.

The graceful bend of the handlebars follows the line of the frame and the single enclosed spring suspension on the leading-axle front forks and the wide and well-sprung tractor-style leather saddle absorbed at least some jarring and jolting from the pot-holed roads. A single Schebler carburetor fed fuel mixture to the four cylinders from a branched manifold. The long cylindrical fuel tank held oil at the rear, and a smaller separate tank mounted under the handlebars held acetylene for lighting. Foot pedals activated a small rear brake, but the with a top speed of around 60mph emergency stops were not advisable. The well-executed design and high quality of manufacture ensured the Henderson quickly became one of the most coveted production motorcycles for riders who wanted a reliable and comfortable machine for covering longer distances in style.

William "Bill" Henderson constantly refined his design and each year of production included improvements and new features, including increased capacity and power. The big 1000cc engine with overhead inlet and side exhaust valves produced almost double the power of the highly-priced 4hp Pierce. Starting was generally trouble-free, with a neat folding hand crank, and the horizontally-split aluminium engine cases were all but leak free. The drawback of all inline four cylinder designs is that all but the front cylinder are screened from the cooling breeze. It was to be almost half a century before

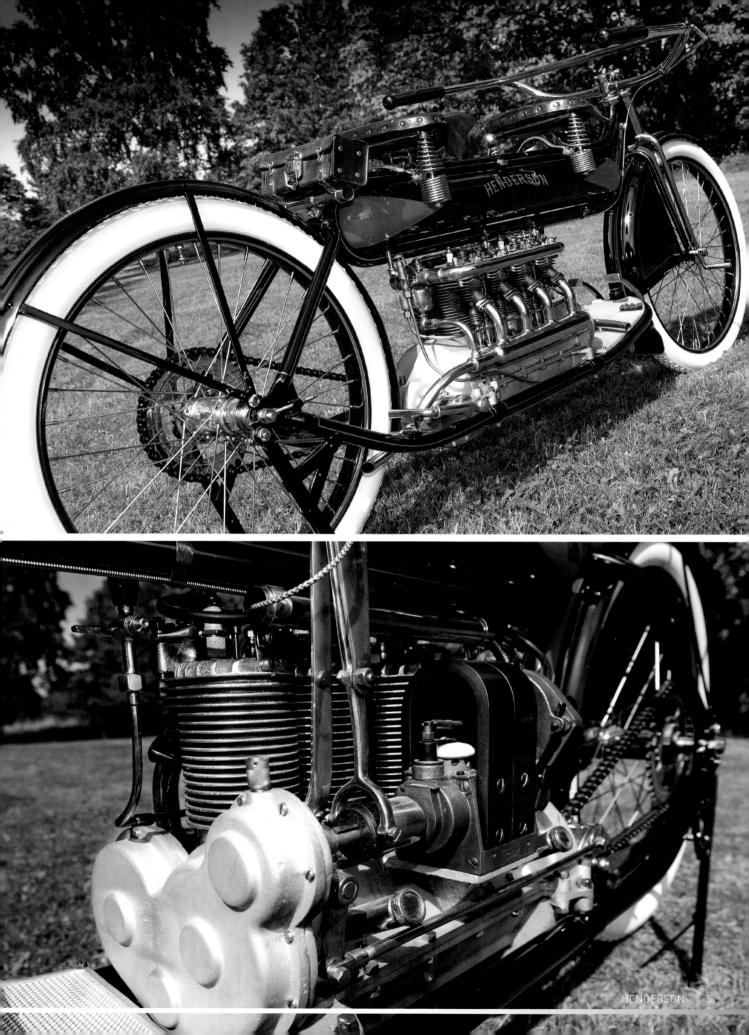

innovations in casting and machining technology made it possible to mass-produce comparatively lightweight four cylinder engines that could sit across the frame ensuring all the cylinders stood an equal chance of shedding surplus heat. Water-cooling, already tried by Major Henry Capel Lofft Holden in 1899 on an interesting four-cylinder engine with horizontally-opposed pairs, was ruled out due to excessive weight. Weight was a big consideration for William and Tom Henderson. Around a decade earlier, while Tom had been working as a salesman at the same car company as his father, a Winton had been driven across America, with a hugely beneficial impact on sales. Both Tom and William knew that sales of their motorcycles relied on capturing the public's imagination and, in order to do that, both speed and reliability were critical. Their efforts were rewarded by an epic circumnavigation of the globe on a Henderson by Carl Stearns Clancy in 1912. Clancy covered something like 18,000 miles in less than a year across all kinds of terrain and in every type of weather and environment. It was an heroic achievement, by both machine and rider, and sales ballooned in response.

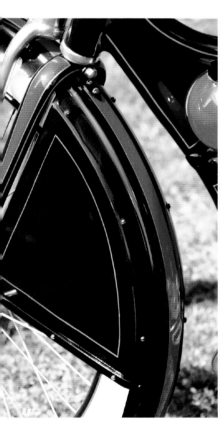

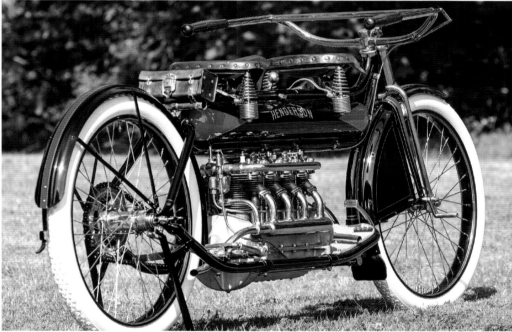

The Depression forced the sale of the business in 1917 to Ignaz Schwinn, who sought to cut costs and broaden appeal by switching to a side-valve engine design under the Excelsior name in Chicago. Bill Henderson didn't want to compromise and soon left to start ACE, where he continued to develop his four cylinder layout. Hendersons continued to be built with larger capacity engines capable of speeds up to 100mph which made them popular with police forces, until production ended in 1931. Aged just 40, Bill was killed test-riding in 1922 but his legacy continued, influencing ACE and, later, Indian motorcycles, right up to the Second World War.

Indian Board Track Racer 1913 *USA*

Engine:	V-twin, 8v four stroke
Valves:	OHV
Capacity:	61cu / 1000cc
Power:	Not known
Top Speed:	100mph / 160kph

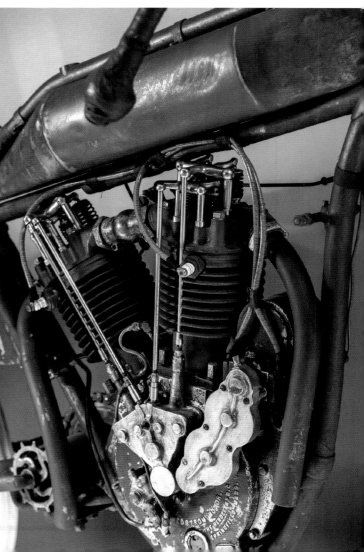

It's unusual to find an example of an early Indian racing motorcycle in such good unrestored condition. Increasingly, for many collectors of early motorcycles the genuine patina of age showing all the scars of battles on the race track and the idiosyncrasies of various owners' modifications is far preferable to the artificial sparkle of a pristine restoration.

Indian is well known today as the manufacturer of highly-prized and distinctive V-twin overhead and side-valve and in-line four-cylinder motorcycles that were produced from the famous factory on State Street, Springfield, Massachusetts, during the inter-war years of the 1920s and 30s, including the much-loved Scout, the Police Scout, the Chief and 1200cc Big Chief. What is often overlooked is that as early 1911, Indian motorcycles were already a world sensation. Over 35,000 motorcycles left the Hendee factory in 1913, and demand was almost doubling year on year, driven not only by racing victories on the board tracks in America that drew vast crowds of spectators and enthusiasts but also in

part by unprecedented success at the prestigious TT races in England. European motorcyclists were stunned in 1911 when the British riders Oliver Godfrey, Charles Franklin and Arthur Moorhouse took First, Second and Third in the Isle of Man TT on their American designed and built sleeved down 500cc Indian V-twin racers.

The two-speed chain-drive transmission of the Indian machines was to prove a decisive factor in TT races on the mountainous Isle of Man, as was Oscar Hedstrom's proprietary carburettor and the doubling-up of the valves in his overhead valve engine. Racers soon discovered that eight valves made it easier to tune the Indian for greater speed. Fitting four valves rather than two to each of the twin cylinders had the double advantage of facilitating heat dissipation through the larger surface area and a further and very significant by-product was increased reliability, as valve failure due to overheating was greatly reduced.

The vivid red paint residue still visible on the replacement engine of this unrestored example of an American board-racer was the idea of George Hendee who, with his business partner and designer Oscar Hedstrom, produced the first 'red' Indian at the turn of the century. Their first production model, a 'Thor' engined single-cylinder machine, scooped first, second and third in the New York to Boston endurance trial of 1902, ridden by the two manufacturers themselves and George Holden, gaining the fledgling factory valuable public attention.

Single cylinder engines dominated the limited production until the first V-twin Indian appeared in 1907, based largely on the single, and built around a narrow 42 degree engine with the rear cylinder, as in the single cylinder machine, forming the rear seat tube of the frame. This arrangement was dropped in 1909 with the introduction of V-twin inlet-over-exhaust Indians in 5.5hp and 988cc 7hp with loop frames and leaf spring forks.

But it was the eight-valve V-twin released in 1911 that really caught the motorcycling public's attention, immediately securing wins and publicity on the board-tracks across America and establishing the name of Indian Motorcycles around the world.

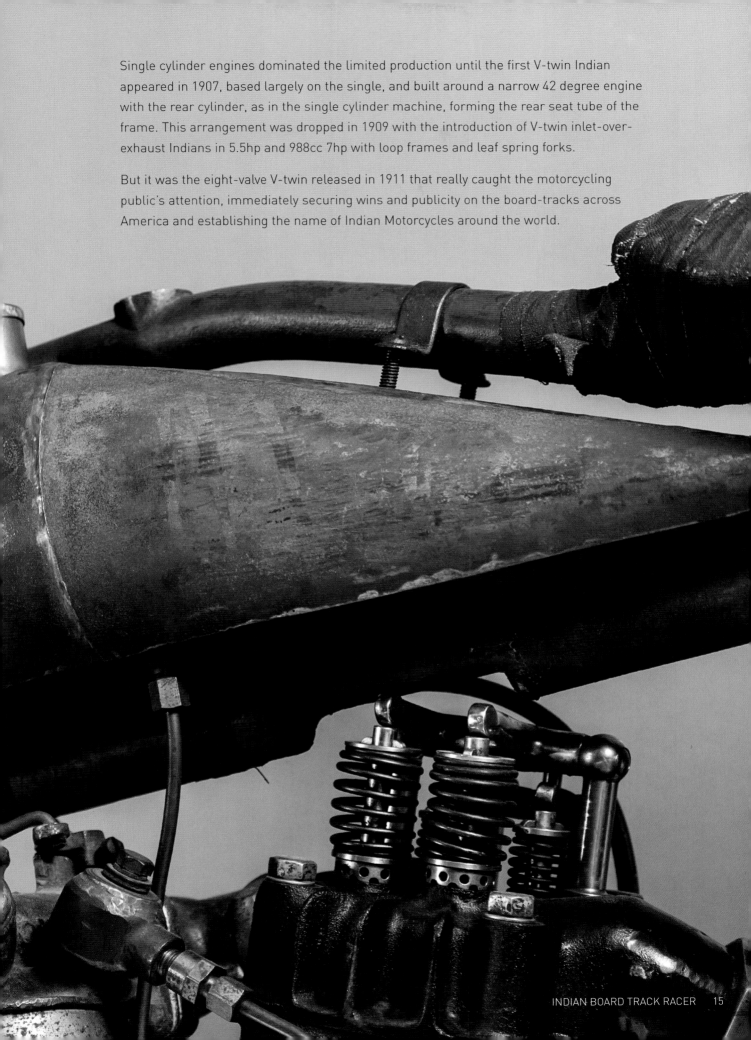

Flying Merkel 1914 USA

Engine:	V-twin
Valves:	Inlet over exhaust
Capacity:	61cu / 1000cc
Power:	6-7hp / 4-5kw
Top Speed:	60mph / 100kph

In the drab days when Henry Ford's company promised you a car in any colour as long as it was black, the vivid colour-schemes of American motorcycles like the 1911 Flying Merkel must have screamed speed and excitement like blazing comets from outer space. The dazzling exuberance of design and colour flashes-forwards to the 1950s and must have left bystanders staring open-mouthed at the side of the road in the early days of motorised transport. With its eye-catching white tyres and liberal plating to the engine, exhausts and cycle parts, the Merkel had plenty of show as well as go. The brand name is emblazoned in bold on the sides of the fuel tank in a typeface that suggests the wonder of the carnival or circus ring.

Joe Merkel was building single cylinder motorcycles as early as 1902. The Miami Cycle and Manufacturing Company of Ohio took over the business in 1911, following racing successes by Maldwyn Jones, who beat the champion 'Canonball Baker' in a ten mile race on a Flying Merkel. Margaret Gast, the incredible 'Mile a Minute Girl', also rode a Merkel.

The Flying Merkel is a robust machine with the V-twin engine supported in a strong loop frame, the large diameter front tube canted forward to give front wheel clearance and facilitate a relaxed steering geometry. In many ways the Flying Merkel was light years ahead of its time. Pared-down functionality and a focus on weight-saving is evident in every carefully thought-out part including the engine cases in light alloy, ribbed for strength to cope with relentless full-bore running with wide-open throttles

on roads or race tracks. In response to the rutted, bumpy roads, Joe Merkel designed and patented a sprung front fork that could be seen as the forerunner of the telescopic fork, calling it the "Truss Fork" and prompting the slogan, 'the next thing to flying' which gave the Merkel its famous name. Merkel's revolutionary rear suspension arrangement with the pivot coinciding with the drive chain axis to keep a constant tension regardless of suspension travel predates a similar idea employed by celebrated aftermarket frame builder Bimota by over half a century.

The Merkel was supplied in different engine sizes, with both 54ci and 61ci displacements available, giving 6 or 7 hp which on the roads of the time and with the comparatively rudimentary rear wheel braking was probably considered quite sufficient. The engine was rugged and hard wearing, using ball-bearings instead of bronze bushes as was the more common practice at the time. It was lubricated by an innovative throttle-controlled oiling system introduced by Joe Merkel that many years later was copied by Indian, Harley Davidson and others.

Starting the Merkel was down to hard pedalling but once on the move the motorcycle was capable of relaxed long distance cruising with two speeds and the wide and proud handlebars giving the rider plenty of leverage. The exhaust is elegantly routed from both cylinders and joins before dropping down below the rear swing arm. The motor breathes in through a single Schebler carburettor with a big-bore double manifold.
The racing version of the Flying Merkel ran with chain drive rather than a belt and no brakes, and was a celebrated sight on the racetracks of the time. Production of the iconic Flying Merkel ended just before America's involvement in the Great War.

Engine:	V twin ohv
Weight:	340lbs / 154kg
Capacity:	60cu / 988cc
Power:	45hp / 34kw
Top Speed:	100mph / 160kph

ALPINE GRAND SPORTS

Brough Superior

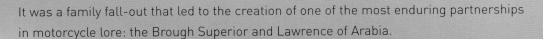

It was a family fall-out that led to the creation of one of the most enduring partnerships in motorcycle lore: the Brough Superior and Lawrence of Arabia.

George Brough had been working for his father and riding Brough motorcycles for many years before a rift in family relations caused him to leave the family business to set up on his own in Nottingham in 1919, adding 'Superior' to the name.

The Brough Superior was to become known as the 'Rolls Royce of Motorcycles' and is perhaps even more prized and sought after today as it was in its heyday. Regarded by many as the 'first superbike', the cachet of the Brough Superior brand has been enhanced over the years by its association with T.E. Lawrence who, in the unlikely guise of 'Aircraftsman Shaw', owned seven examples of the marque between the wars, until he infamously rode one into immortality in 1935, killed when swerving to avoid a couple of schoolboys on their bicycles. It's said that the disagreement between George and

his father that led to the parting of their ways was over engine configuration; William was convinced opposed flat twins were the future, and George, having ridden V-Twins himself, followed his own path. It's an argument that continues to this day between different brands and supporters of both layouts.

Brough model numbers were supposed to refer to their top speed and the rakish lines with high-level exhausts and gleaming nickel-plated meteor-shaped tank suggest the SS100 is capable of everything claimed for it and more. Released in 1924, each machine came with a certificate confirming it had run at 100mph in testing. In the same year, Brough set no fewer than 9 speed records, including a solo 123mph.

The deep black coach enamel over heavy nickel plating reeks of class and quality and the 988cc JAP V Twin engine was in effect an overhead valve upgrade of the well trusted SS80 sidevalve powerplant that had powered George's own Brough, "Spit and Polish", to victory Brookland's at over 100mph as well as over 200 other races and hill climbs. The Alpine Sport SS100 was named after George's gold medal in the Alpine Rally.

A larger capacity, stroked 995cc engine was to follow, as well as a Pendine model, named after Pendine Sands where the speed trials were held, which claimed a 110mph top speed. The SS100 featured exposed overhead valves with pushrods and rocker arms and a three-speed hand-change gearbox. The frame had a rigid rear end, although the SS100 was later offered with suspension with a single spring under the seat dampening a cantilever rear fork.

It could be argued that the Brough SS100 is a 'special' rather than a production model, as apart from the frame and tank, George sourced most of the major components from other maunufacturers: the engines from JAP and later Matchless, the brakes from Royal Enfield, the Castle forks a revision of a Harley Davidson design, and gearboxes from Sturmey Archer and Norton. Custom builders are still emulating the pared-down V-twin look that George Brough pioneered over a century ago. Being a competition rider, as well as a mechanic, meant that George had a unique eye and feel for combining components in a way that produced a machine that was far more than the sum of its parts, but this also put him at a disadvantage when it came to negotiating with his suppliers. Speed came at a high premium, then as now, and the onset of the Second World War brought production to a final halt.

Lawrence of Arabia on his Brough Superior.

Harley-Davidson
Peashooter 1926 *USA*

Engine:	Ohv single cylinder twin-port.
Valves:	Overhead valve
Weight:	187lbs / 85kg
Capacity:	21cu / 346 cc
Power:	20hp / 15kw
Top Speed:	80mph / 130kph

The spritely 350cc ohv Harley-Davidson hurtled around oval board-tracks and into the history books in the mid 1920s, thrilling huge crowds all around the world who gathered to see the elbow-to-elbow expoits of their racing heroes.

The single-cyliner works ohv racing version of the side-valve 350cc machine that Harley-Davidson marketed around the world as an alternative to its larger capacity V-twins in the financially constrained years between the wars became very popular with racers and spectators alike for its speed and reliability. Sawn-off twin exhaust pipes, a feature of many single-cylinder sporting machines of the period, gave the unsilenced machine a distinctive exhaust note and it was quickly dubbed the 'Peashooter'.

Harley-Davidson are renowned today throughout the world for their V-twins but the first machine produced by the company in 1904 was a 500cc single, the 'Silent Grey Fellow'. Having built inlet-over-exhaust V-twins in the early twenties, Harley-Davidson introduced its range of new single-cylinder models in 1926 partly in response to the success Indian Motorcycles had been enjoying with sales of its own single cylinder machine, the Prince.

The road-going version of the Harley-Davidson 350cc ohv single was not a big seller, and the less expensive to produce, easier to service side-valve 350cc proved more popular, not least due to its claim of 80 miles per gallon fuel economy in a time of growing austerity. A complete decoke of the side-valve, including removal and replacement of the licensed Ricardo-designed cylinder head, was advertised by Harley-Davidson as being a twenty minute job that 'anyone can do' and the technical experience gained on the 350cc side valve single was later to be applied directly to the 750cc and 1200cc V-twins.

In its olive green livery, a hangover from the switch from grey in 1917 as Harley-Davidson prepared to join the war in Europe, the Peashooter was understated in appearance by comparison with some of its contemporaries,

but if the paint scheme was conservative, the performance of the ohv motor was anything but, and the Harley-Davidson soon came to dominate the short American dirt tracks. The high-revving motor was fuelled with a mixture of alcohol and benzol, fed into the high compression cylinder through the Wheeler Schebler Model G carburettor. Respectable power, combined with low weight, gave the board-racer punchy acceleration. The ohv engine was purpose-built for racing at sustained high speeds of up to 90 miles an hour. Two low mounted camshafts drove the valvetrain via pushrods, and the motor sported a natrium cooled exhaust valve and force feed lubrication. Ignition was supplied by a magneto set to the rear of the engine. While road-going versions of the Peashooter came with three gears, racers had only a countershaft. The other major difference was the rigid frame, which was slightly shorter for the racing bikes, with more lively steering, and the sprung front fork. Both the little singles shared the attractive new teardrop tank shape that had been introduced on the V-twins.

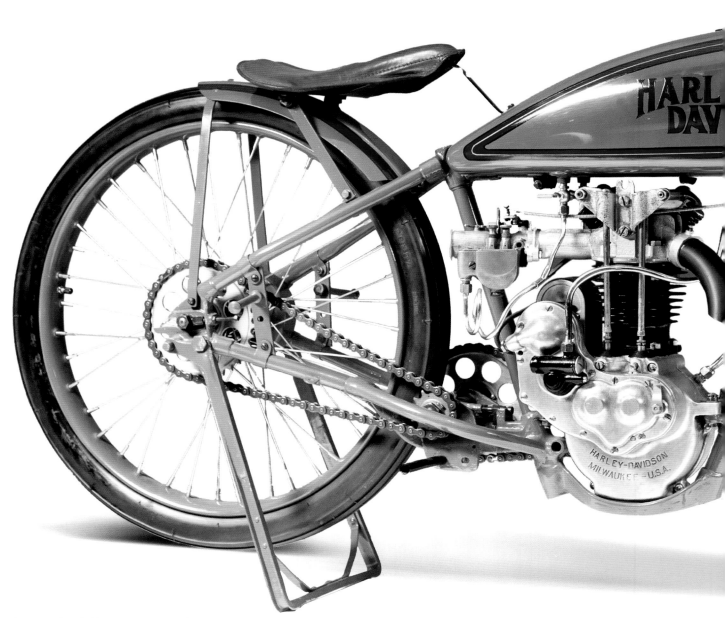

Joe Petrali famously raced the Peashooter for Harley-Davidson to countless wins and championships in the twenties and thirties and proved beyond argument that the 350cc ohv was a full works racer that an amateur rider could buy over the counter and race very competitively, even against far larger capacity side-valve and ohv V-twin machines. Production of the Peashooter was ended in 1934 by the economic crisis of the depression.

Joe Petrali on his Harley-Davidson Peashooter.

Folke Mannerstedt (second from the left) with his Husqvarna race team 1931.

Husqvarna 500 cc Single 1931 SWEDEN

Engine:	1-cyl JAP
Valves:	Overhead valve
Capacity:	30cu / 500 cc
Power:	35hp / 26kw

While it had produced motorcycles very successfully for the military during the First World War, the Husqvarna factory in Sweden decided to direct considerable effort towards racing in order to win vital civilian sales between the wars. Folke Mannerstedt joined Husqvarna in 1928 and was a gifted young Swedish motorcycle racer and mechanical engineer who was tasked with leading the company's racing efforts. He had developed his motorcycle design skills at the famous FN company in Belgium that had supplied single cylinder 1.25hp engines for Husqvarna motorcycles from as early as 1903.

Working with the highly talented technician Calle Heimdahl, Mannerstedt set out to build a 500cc racer that would be capable of challenging at Grand Prix level. Mannerstedt and the Husqvarna management team were unsure which direction to take; the company already produced a very popular V-twin with their own side-valve 550cc engine, loosely inspired by the Swiss Moto-Reve engines they had used in machines developed for army use. However the most successful road-racing models of the time were largely British single-cylinder machines, with overhead camshaft Nortons in particular taking wins in many championships. Mannerstedt intended to build a Husvqarna V-twin GP racer, but while designing it, the design team also built and tuned a succession of single-cylinder 250cc and 500cc racers, using British made JAP and Sturmey Archer engines, partly in order to study in depth the leading side valve and overhead valve technology and design that was proving so successful on the race track. Mannerstedt hedged his bets, and the development of a V-twin and the single cylinder racers ran in parallel, with research and tuning effort being shared between the two projects. At the 1930 Swedish GP in Saxtorp, Husqvarna entered a selection of models; the incredible 500cc V-twin, two different versions of the JAP-powered 500cc single, and a 250cc JAP engined single.

Low, slender and fast, the big V-twin won the day, with Yngve Eriksson bringing it in third, ahead of the singles. The frame-filling fifty degree V-Twin 500cc Husqvarna engine produced excellent torque and to offset any disadvantage to the European and British racing singles, the weight was pared down to a minimum by the early use of light alloy for the two sets of barrels and heads. The sheer size and layout of the engine dictated frame and girder fork geometry, contributing to handling that struggled to contain the power of the motor. A similar problem was encountered with the 500cc single; Mannerstedt's success in wringing power from the JAP motor had produced over 31hp at 6,000 rpm and the rigid frame and relatively simple Webb front fork suspension struggled to keep handling in step with performance.

A frame brace was added to the single-cylinder machine in an attempt to rectify the problem, running the length of the motorcycle from the base of the steering head all the way back on either side to the very back of the frame. Without realising it, Mannerstedt had foreshadowed the full duplex cradle that Cromie and Rex McCandless were to design for Norton in 1949 as was to become famous as the 'featherbed' frame. The V-twin was taken forward as the GP racer, becoming hugely successful and winning every year at Saxtorp between 1932 and 1935, while the 500cc single continued very successful in road races and off-road events. The Husqvarna became extremely successful in the early 1930's hillclimbs in Sweden, a form of competition in which you drove up a winding track on a very steep hill. Swedish stars such as Ragge Sunnqvist, Gunnar Kallén and Martin Strömberg among others were the top riders in hillclimbs at Klevaliden and Klintabacken.

Crocker Big tank 1939 *USA*

Engine:	V-twin
Valves:	Overhead valve
Capacity:	61cu / 1000 cc
Power:	50hp / 37kw

Indian dealer and speedway race tuner Albert Crocker set out to capture the market by producing a motorcycle that would be superior in performance and build quality to anything else available in America for the road.

Albert Crocker rode for 'Thor' before he followed Thor-manufactured engines to Indian Motorcycles, where he dreamed of one day designing his own motorcycle, and the motorcycle that bears his name is strongly influenced by his racing experience. From 1931 he built aftermarket racing frames for Indian Scout V twin engines, that were particularly successful with his overhead-valve tuning conversion for Indian engines. In 1933 he produced his own single-cylinder engined racer that competed with varying success against Harley Davidson and JAP engined machines. Al had also raced JAP engined machines on the board tracks and recognising some of the technical advantages of the European engines that had been

set out by the talented Val Page, Al Crocker teamed up with racer 'P.A.' Bigsby to hand-build a new V-twin road model incorporating many of the design principles that had given JAP-engined machines the edge on the track.

The big 1000cc Crocker was the only overhead valve road V-twin machine available in America when it was launched, appearing well before the Harley Davidson 'Knucklehead', it was designed to look like a full-bore track racer, leaner, lighter, and more compact than the competition. Even when the Knucklehead was launched, it was slower than the Crocker. The engine was a unique 61ci 45 degree 60bhp V-twin of hemi-head design to begin with, followed by vertical-valve heads after 1936. The rakish hard-tail frame was designed with an impeccable racing pedigree from Al Crocker's racing days. Suspension came in the form of girder type forks and a big tractor-style sprung saddle. High handlebars, a hand gear shift and running boards gave the Crocker a relaxed western appearance, although many were 'bobbed' after the war, losing their mudguards or 'fenders' and being stripped down to their racing essentials for the street.

Advertisements of the time claimed the Crocker was 'ideal for those who like to tangle on the highway' and when he launched his hand-built, individually finished creation, Al Crocker provocatively offered with it a personal guarantee that he would give a full refund if a

Crocker failed to outgun any stock Harley or Indian on the highway. Myth maintains he never had to pay out. Less well known perhaps is that Al Crocker lost money on just about every one of the small number of motorcycles he produced. The few Crockers that were built between 1936 and 1942, less than a hundred in all, were all built as one-offs, the company even advertising that every Crocker motor was a "bench job". Crocker had to work extremely hard to stay in front of the competition, constantly introducing innovations like constant mesh gearboxes, large capacity aluminium petrol tanks, but where he led, other manufacturers like Indian and Harley Davidson were able to copy at a discounted price. Crocker customers could have their machine built to a personal specification and request larger capacity engines by having the cylinders bored out, or a unique colour scheme, but bragging rights on the highway came at a very high price, and when war loomed, as with many motorcycle businesses of the time, the order book emptied and the company stopped production.

The Crocker still looks astonishingly contemporary, as many modern custom and production V-twins seek to recapture the pared-back board-racer look. Only about half the original Los Angeles built Crockers survive, but it's still possible to build a Crocker today from scratch using entirely new-manufactured parts.

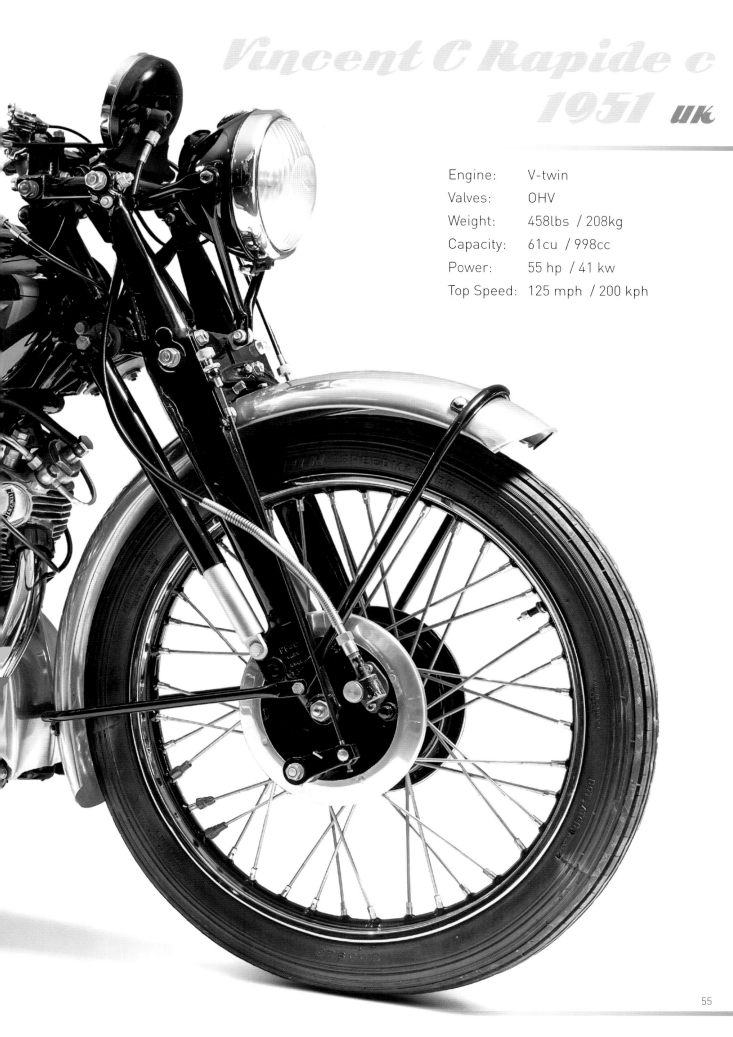

Engine:	V-twin
Valves:	OHV
Weight:	458lbs / 208kg
Capacity:	61cu / 998cc
Power:	55 hp / 41 kw
Top Speed:	125 mph / 200 kph

The Vincent can be seen as taking up the British V-twin baton from Brough in the years running up to the Second World War. Phil Vincent bought the HRD brand out of liquidation from Howard Raymond Davies in 1927 but it wasn't until another Phil, the Australian designer Phil Irving, joined the business in 1932 that new models with proprietary engines were produced in time for a launch at Olympia in 1934.

This was a 500cc single ohv model with a high cam and the story goes that Phil Irving conceived the design for what was to become the famous Vincent V-twin design by overlaying two design drawings of the single-cylinder engine on his desk. In a moment of genius Irving realised that by creating a new crankcase, he could employ all the other major components of their single-cylinder engine without any changes and build a V-twin model for minimum development costs.

Despite racing Vincent HRD machines with their new single engine performing well at the 1935 TT, money and materials were both in short supply, and the two Phils set out to use creative thought to solve manufacturing problems and reduce cost wherever possible on the new twin.

The downside was that the original single-cylinder design had been rather rushed, pulled together in less than three months, and some of the shortcomings of that design were carried through into the design for the first pre-war incarnation V-Twin. It was released in 1936, as the Series A Rapide, and while it was billed as being 'the fastest production machine on two, three or four wheels' with a top speed of 108mph, faster even than the JAP-powered Brough SS100, the HRD, as it was still known, soon gained the derogatory nick-name, 'The Plumber's Nightmare' due to over-complicated and leak-prone external oil and fuel piping. Without the outbreak of war, the Vincent story might well have ended there.

Vincent moved into a second factory in Stevenage following the war and soon after the heavily refined and rethought Series B was unveiled, with a revised engine design of 50 degrees angle instead of the earlier 47.5 degrees, and more power and speed. Every part of the new Vincent was meticulously designed around its purpose. Most revolutionary was their decision to dispense with the traditional tubular cradle-type frame altogether to save on steel which was scarce and expensive after the war. In their quest for perfection Phil Vincent and Phil Irving delighted in making one part serve two functions, as evidenced by their pioneering use of the engine as a stressed member; instead of bolting the motor into a frame as was standard practice, Vincent and Irving turned the concept on its head and hung all the cycle parts from the strong unit-construction engine and gearbox of the 1000cc Rapide, saving weight and increasing rigidity. A strong sheet-steel 'spine' connects the cylinder heads and supports the front wheel and forks. This box-section spine, hidden beneath the fuel tank, also doubles up as the oil reservoir

for the engine. Oil supply was neater, with enclosed valve gear. The big advance in handling was in the reduced wheel base, made possible by the absence of any front down tube, which meant that despite the bulk of its 1000cc V-twin engine, weight was not excessive and the Vincent was far more maneuverable than rival machines of similar capacity.

The new model also featured a beefed-up gearbox and clutch to put down all the torque and power onto the road. The rear suspension, an ingenious triangulated swinging-arm with the damping under the seat, is slung from the rear of the engine. Wherever possible components on the Vincent serve more than one purpose. The seat pan is also the tool box, the rear mudguard stay swings down to become a rear stand, the mudguard itself hinges up to allow easy removal of the rear wheel. The devil is in the detail; apparently adding unnecessary weight, small cross-bars on the end of the wheel spindles actually save carrying a much heavier spanner that could be lost or forgotten just when needed. Racing at the TT and Clubmans events confirmed the Vincent twin's fame and the Black Shadow model of 1948 with black painted engine cases was essentially a race-tuned upgrade of the Rapide. The Series C Black Lightning, was also added to the line-up in 1948, with tweaks to cam timing, compression and carburation as well as gear ratios and the girdraulic forks and rear suspension to create an out-and-out fully-tuned over-the-counter racer. Big, burly, but with considered poise, the Vincent was an early superbike that continued to feature on rostrums even into the 1970s, long after production ceased in the mid 1950s.

BMW Rennsport RS54
1954 GERMANY

Engine:	DOHC Boxer 2 cylinder
Capacity:	30cu / 496cc
Power:	45 bhp / 34kw
Weight:	286lbs / 130kg

Following the Second World War, the FIM allowed BMW to return to racing with normally-aspirated racing engines as opposed to their all-conquering World Land Speed Record -holding supercharged machines of the inter-war years. A dedicated DOHC racing machine, the RS54 was made available to those very few private racers who could afford it and in total, only about two dozen of the highly-advanced machines were ever built.

In its classic BMW black livery with white pinstripes, the RS54 didn't look so different; in fact the design represented a total rethink of everything BMW had produced in the past, from the clockwise spinning of the crankshaft, the reverse of all other BMW engines. This was revolution masquerading as evolution.

The RS54 Rennsport, launched in 1953, was a total redesign of the traditional BMW two-cylinder opposed 'boxer' engine layout, while retaining broad BMW engineering practice that continue to this day, with a crankshaft running on three bearings in a one-piece aluminium crankcase driving con-rods and 8:1 pistons inside stubby finned aluminium cylinders, aircooled on either side of the motorcycle. The engine dimensions started at 66mm x 72mm giving a displacement of 492cc and subsequent racing development took the engine over 'square' through 68 x 68 to 70 x 64 mm, breathing through a pair of 30mm Amal-Fischer TT carburettors

The RS54 engine was complemented by a radically updated full-loop frame in an effort to improve handling in response to the legendary Norton 'Featherbed' frame, as fitted to the Manx and International models. The new BMW frame was a masterful creation of lug-less integrity in all-welded tubing and the unflexing rear swing-arm held a single-leading shoe brake and braced the trademark BMW driveshaft extending from the flywheel clutch and four or five-speed gearbox.

Rear suspension was by a pair of fully hydraulic dampers, dramatically improving handling over previous models. The front suspension followed the Earles-type design which was patented in 1953 by Englishman Ernie Earles and adopted by MV Agusta for a time for weight-saving and strength, and anchored a chunky 200mm twin-leading shoe front brake.

The low centre of gravity achieved by engine layout and frame design, combined with a relatively low weight of 130kg and respectable power output of 45bhp should have put the predictable, sweet-handling RS54 BMW back on the podium at tracks all around Europe, but in reality, instability at high speed on long open tracks remained an issue and only a handful of gifted riders such as Zeller were able to realise its potential.

MV Agusta Monoalbero Corsa 1954 ITALY

Engine:	Single cylinder
Valves:	Single overhead camshaft
Weight:	210lbs / 95kg
Capacity:	7.5cu / 123.5cc
Power:	14hp / 10kw

Designed by the maestro, Ing. Piero Remor, of Gilera fame and related in spirit at least to the all-conquering double-knocker works 125cc and the larger four cylinder machines for which MV is perhaps best known, the sohc MV Sport Compezione is a jewel of a motorcycle.

In the famous 'fire engine' red factory colour of Count Domenico Agusta's motorcyle business, Meccanica Verghera, named after the location in Gallerate north of Milan, the 125 was built as an over-the-counter track bike.

The 125cc class was highly popular in Italy in the late 1940s with two strokes from companies like Morini setting the pace. Mondial introduced a dohc four stroke 125, designed by Alfonso Drusiani that convinced Remor and his mechanic, Arturo Magni, that he should design a similar machine for MVs works team. The four stroke dohc works racer produced 17 bhp and was very successful; Cecil Sandford and MV won the 125cc World Championship in 1952. A sohc 125cc production racer was produced that customers could buy and emulate the great MV works riders, Sandford, Carlo Ubbiali and Les Graham. While the production racer shared the 53x56 mm bore and stroke of the works bike, the power developed by the sohc engine was far lower at around 14 bhp at 10,000 rpm.

The launch of the single-cam 125cc production racer was overshadowed by the tragic death of Les Graham who was tragically killed racing the MV 500cc four cylinder machine in the Senior TT at the Isle of Man in 1953, just after winning the 125cc race. The works dohc 125 was fast and light at around 210lbs and went on to win the world Championship again in 1955 ridden by Ubbiali and 1956, when he also won the 250cc class on a bored-out 63 x 69mm version of the 125cc machine with a capacity of 203cc and 27bhp.

Other than the simpler, single cam arrangement, the production racer was very similar in many respects to the dohc works machine. The bottom-ends of the two engines were virtually identical, with dry sump and gear-driven oil pump, although the twin-cam engine was fitted with a five speed gearbox, the production machine having only four gears. The two models shared the same frame, thin racing seat and fuel tank, sculpted to enable the rider to tuck well in. The front forks with their clever single spring and damper layout, rear suspension units, front and rear brakes were also common to both motorcycles although the equipment supplied to works machines was carefully selected, balanced and

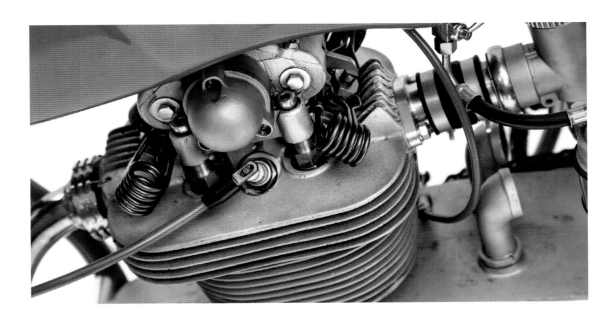

tuned by Magni's race mechanics. The sohc breathed in through a rubber mounted 27mm Dell'Orto carburettor, and out through an elegant chromed megaphone running back along the left hand side of the machine and canted up slightly from just under the footpeg to give ground clearance on cornering. The magneto sits at the front of the engine cases, protected and cooled in a cast aluminium housing forward of the multi-plate clutch. The elongated cover down the right of the heavily finned cylinder contains the stacked gears for the camshaft. To the rear of the engine, slung on the right hand side of the frame under the racing saddle is the sweeping curve of the large oil tank.

The Monoalbero Corsa was to launch the careers of many young racers, perhaps none more significant than that of Mike Hailwood in his very first race at Oulton Park in 1957, where he took his 125cc sohc to 11th place behind winner Cecil Sandford, MV's great world champion, who rather ironically, that day rode a Mondial.

AJS 7R Racer 1960 *UK*

Engine:	1-cyl
Valves:	Overhead camshaft
Capacity:	21cu / 350 cc
Power:	41.5 hp / 31kw

For many, the AJS 7R remains one of the most handsome motorcycles ever produced. Designed by Philip Walker, the 350cc 7R was conceived as a motorcycle specifically designed for racing and campaigning by the enthusiastic privateer. Low, lean, with a reserved simplicity of line that suggests effortless speed, the popular 7R came to be known affectionately as the 'Boy Racer' and was the ride of choice for many short-circuit and TT riders. Though it never won a TT, Bob McIntyre secured the 7R's place in Isle of Man history in 1952 when he won the Junior Manx Grand Prix and then two days later took the same bike to second place in the Senior against larger capacity 500cc machines.

The single-cylinder design of the 7R could not be more traditional or conservative; even the staid colour scheme of black and gold is in keeping with the finish of pinstriped pre-war gentleman's motorcycles. The protective gold paint on the engine is not just decorative, however, it signals a high magnesium content and therefore ultra-low weight. The 7R was designed and built to be competitive from the start on short circuit race tracks the world over and appealed to many clubman riders because its sturdy engine was easy to set up and keep in tune compared with rival and more complex machinery like the Norton. You could race the 7R at the weekend, stick it back in the shed or garage and it would only need a quick fettle and check over before the next race meeting.

For those riders who wanted to push the boundaries and experiment in the dark arts of squish and port-polishing for improved gas flow to tweak the motor for that important edge over the competition, the single-cylinder 7R was a relatively straightforward piece of engineering. Armed with an oil-smudged copy of P.E. Irving's 'Tuning For Speed' and the will to win, privateer racers could tinker away through the winter nights in the quest for a few more vital horsepower or a mile or two extra on the top speed. Amateur tuning efforts often led to increased fuel consumption and the later examples of the 7R came with a larger petrol tank to avoid the frustration of pushing a machine back to the pits. "To finish first, first you have to finish" is still the racer's motto and the chain-driven single-overhead cam 7R was essentially a design that had been in production and development since well before the Second World War and was well regarded for its simple reliability. There wasn't a lot to go wrong, and if something did break, spares weren't prohibitively expensive for the privateer on a tight budget.

The 7R is not only an easy machine to fettle, it's also, importantly, a very forgiving ride. It was probably this, more than anything, that made it such a popular motorcycle for those breaking in to racing. Light and responsive, its continued success on the track is largely due to it's frame geometry which gives it excellent and predictable handling characteristics, as anyone who has campaigned an 'Ajay' will testify. The big 8" twin-leading shoe conical front and rear brakes are capable of dropping speed off late into tight corners, and the double cradle frame and single-cylinder design allows the engine and separate gearbox to sit low, keeping the weight and centre of gravity close to the ground but not compromising ground clearance. The stubby megaphone exhaust sweeps tightly around the recessed timing cover to make it possible to crank the bike right over into bends on both sides, and the neutral balance makes it easy to flick the bike back up and take advantage of the torque of the single engine powering into the next straight. The steering angle coupled with efficient telescopic front forks and rear swinging-arm with twin rear shocks gives the rider few surprises and suits a wide variety of circuits.

Racing, it is said, improves the breed, and while the original incarnation of the 7R introduced in 1949 looks at first glance to be near-identical to the very last iteration over ten years later, it had already gone through a process of constant refinement and improvement. That development continues right up to today in classic racing circles and through the use of modern techniques and revolutionary materials keeps the 350cc design that was already decades old in the 'Sixties competitive in both performance and efficiency.

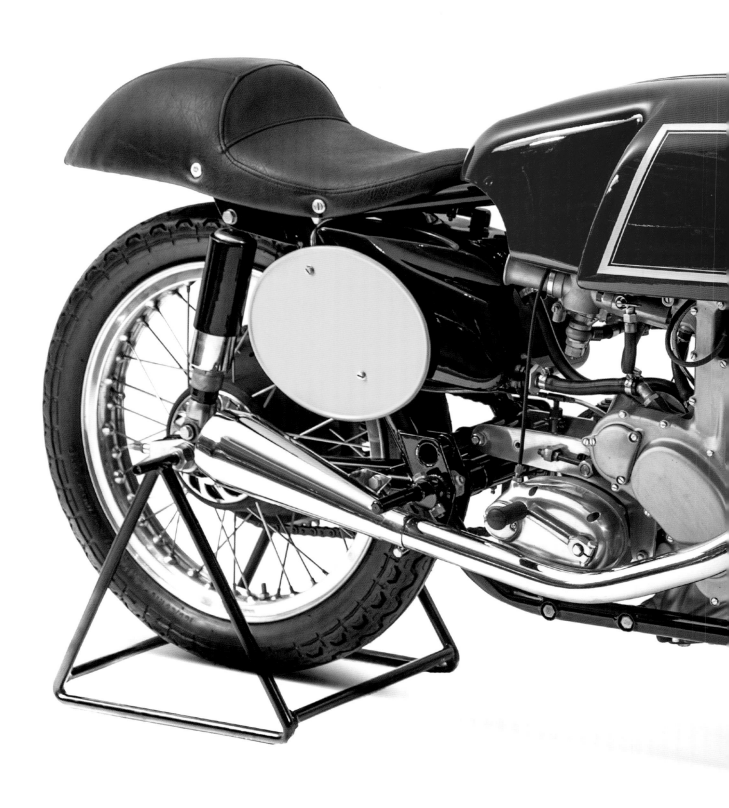

Matchless G50 1962 UK

Engine:	1 cyl. four stroke
Valves:	Overhead camshaft
Capacity:	30cu / 496 cc
Power:	51 hp / 38kw at 7,200 rpm
Top speed:	135mph / 217kmh

By the end of the 1950s the popularity of clubmans racing in Britain and Europe was at a peak, and the 500cc class was a favourite. Back at the start of the decade, the Woolwich-based factory had re-entered the racing world after a hiatus of nearly thirty years with a twin cylinder 500cc machine, the Matchless G45, combining cycle parts from the highly successful AJS 7R and a bespoke racing engine loosely derived from the G9 roadbike, but it had not been a great success. Despite victory in the Manx Grand Prix, problems with rocker failures and oil leaks had given the G45, with its three-bearing crank and separate cylinders and heads, a reputation, perhaps undeserved, for unreliability and over-complexity. This put off a lot of clubman racers who might otherwise have been customers for a viable alternative in the 500cc class to the ubiquitous Manx Norton. Crucially, the G50 was also difficult to ride well by anyone other than a highly skilled rider as the power band was quite narrow.

In an effort to regain the support and custom of the clubman racer, Associated Motor Cycles or AMC launched the single-cylinder G50 in 1958-9. It was essentially a big brother of the AJS 7R, sharing near-identical chassis parts fitted with a bigger 500cc chain-driven single overhead camshaft engine bored out to 90mm but keeping the 350cc machine's stroke of 78mm. At 496cc

and with around 51 bhp on tap at 7,200 revs, the Matchless G50 caught the attention of the racing fraternity from the moment it arrived on the start line.

From a distance, the main distinguishing feature of the Matchless G50 was the maroon painted tank and its winged 'M' logo in contrast to the black with gold pinstriping of the AJS 7R. The engine, with its protective gold coating, looked very similar to the smaller 350cc but in fact on the production bikes the castings were purpose-made.

The duplex cradle frame, big tank, drum brakes, variable-rate 'Teledraulic' forks and Girling rear suspension were all common with the 7R. Overall, the package was familiar, tried and tested and above all, reliable. With larger capacity it was also reasonably fast, right on the heels of the far more complex and expensive to run and maintain Norton 500cc Manx. Many racers simply upgraded from their 350cc machines to the new 500. With a wide powerband the G50 was exceptionally forgiving to the rider and its light weight and nimble handling meant it often held its own in races against far more powerful but heavier and more ponderous competition. It was robust and easy to work on and keep in tune compared with the Manx and spares were less expensive. Between its launch in 1959 and production ending in 1962, around 180 Matchless G50s were built, many being successfully exported around the world.

Combined with the refined handling of the 7R frame and running gear, and with plenty of single-cylinder torque out of the corners on tight club circuits, the G50 quickly established itself on the racetrack as a serious contender in the 500cc classes at circuits around the world.

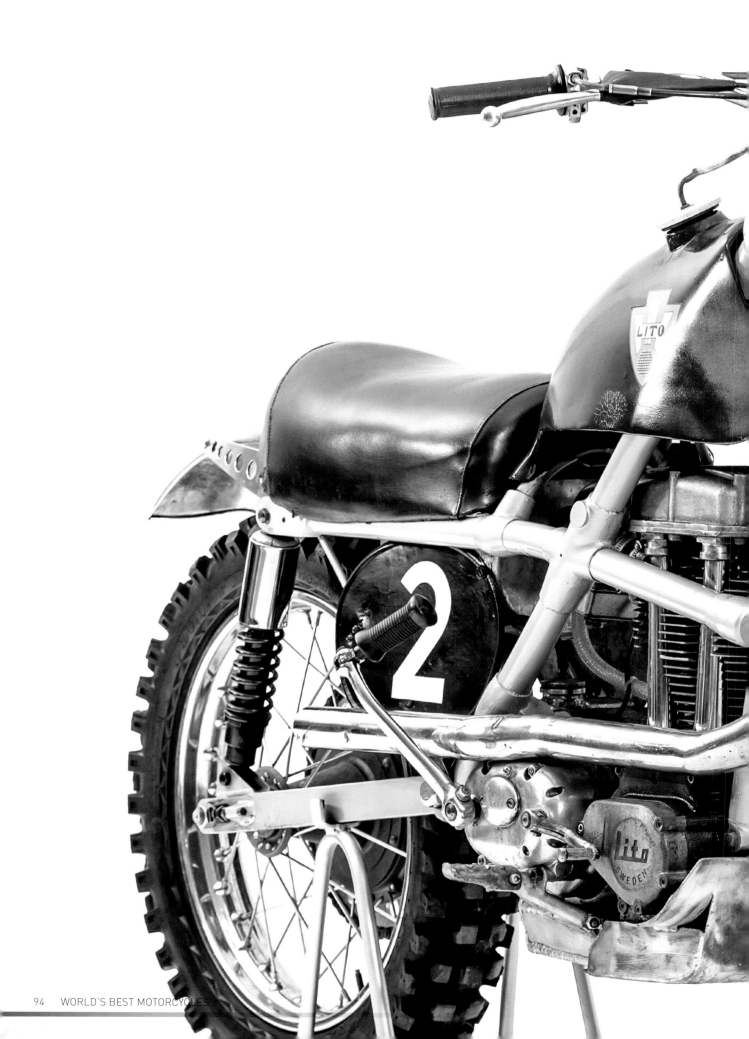

Lito X Cam
1967 *SWEDEN*

Engine:	Single cylinder
Valves:	X Cam
Capacity:	30cu / 496cc
Power:	56bhp / 42kw
Weight:	220lbs / 100kg

In the 1950s, motorcross became hugely popular throughout Europe, and the motorcycles raced were powered by heavy four stroke engines in solidly built frames. The rapid technological advance and rise of the two-stroke, in the mid sixties, led to more lightweight machines that made up for what they lacked in brute power through nimble handling. Almost overnight, the lumbering 500cc four strokes that were fielded by all-conquering factory teams like BSA and had made household names of stars like Les Archer, Rolf Tibblin and Jeff Smith, became virtually obsolete.

Weight was the critical factor to improving handling and acceleration, and a handful of Scandinavian manufacturers, Monark, Husqvarna and Lito sought to defy the inevitable for as long as possible by working to slim down the ageing four-strokes.

Lito, or 'Litoverken', founded in 1958 by the talented Swedish motocross rider Kaj Bornebusch, and named after the Lithography business he owned, was highly successful during what has been called the "Golden Age of Motorcross" between 1957 and 1967, by picking up the baton from the Monark factory team which had shut down after the premature death of its director, Lennart Varborn. Sten Lundin, the star Monark rider, joined Kaj Bornebush at Lito, bringing with him his World Championship-winning ex-Monark works racer, which he continued to race, simply repainted in green Lito colours. Kaj Bornebusch and Lito began to produce similar machines using the same Albin engines as the Monarks. Lundin 'The Viking', and his Lito-badged 500cc Monark won championship after championship in the early sixties, pushing the fledgling Lito factory and brand into the Motocross limelight. The Lito machine, built along very similar lines to the Monark was itself an excellent piece of engineering, aimed purely at the enthusiast rather than mass-market and only some 35 examples were constructed to order between 1961 and 1965 for the top motocross riders of the period including Gunnar Johansson and Bill Nilsson. These heroes of the dirt were fighting a rearguard action against the oncoming tide of the easily-flickable two-stroke and it became obvious that a radical rethink was needed if the four stroke was to have any chance of staying in the running.

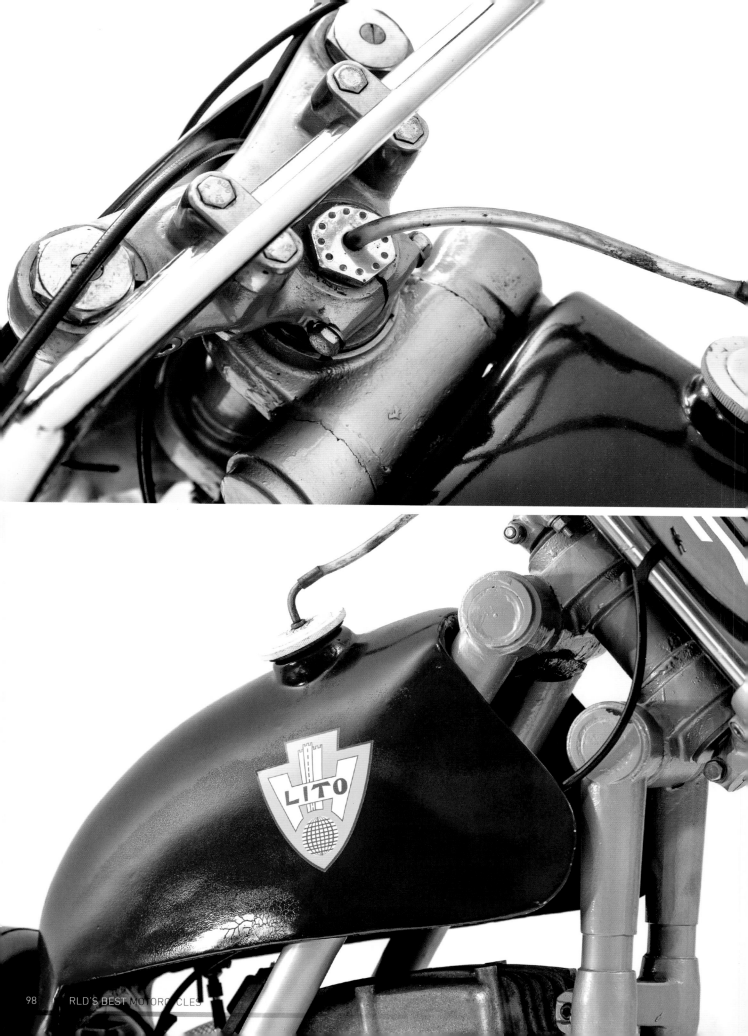

The new Lito X Cam model launched at the Earls Court Motorcycle Show in London in 1966 was a surprise to many, and even caught the highly expert eye of a certain Phil Vincent, of Vincent Motorcycles fame, who wrote of the intriguing Scandinavian creation in *Motorcycle Sport* in February 1967:

"This lonely little exhibit....one solitary machine on the smallest stand at the 1966 show, tucked away at the foot of the escalator leading up to the Gallery... attracted my attention irresistibly... Here was the work of a small group of experienced enthusiasts, who knew what they wanted and were determined to get it, regardless of whether it measured up to the ideas of some stylists or sales manager. The Lito was not designed to appeal except to the qualified engineer or skilled rider. This firm is not aiming for mass sales, rather a few superlative machines a year".

The Lito X Cam was built around a 56hp 500cc engine with a novel design X Cam head, conceived by none other than the legendary Folke Mannerstedt, of FN and Husqvarna fame. Perhaps the most striking exterior element of the new X Cam model was the frame, built in sections and actually bonded together with a Ciba-Geigy product in an obsessive drive to 'add lightness', keeping the weight of the machine down to an incredible 100kg and giving the Lito an impressive power to weight ratio. Compared to the two-stroke opposition however, the new machine was complex and costly to produce, and Litoverken soon hit financial hurdles that it could not overcome; although Staffan Bergmann raced this example of the X Cam, it went quietly into storage half way through its second season, the last hurrah of the Motorcross four-strokes.

Honda CR750
1971 JAPAN

Engine:	4-cyl
Valves:	Overhead camshaft
Capacity:	45cu / 749 cc
Weight:	386lbs / 175kg
Power:	90hp / 67kw
Top Speed:	150mph / 241kph

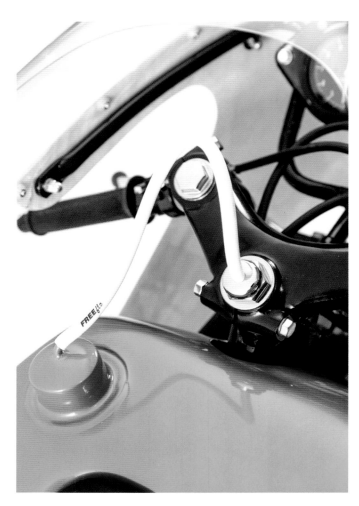

If the launch of the CB750 and victory at the Bol d'Or 24hrs race in 1969 caught the motorcycle world by surprise, Honda's entry in the prestigious Daytona 200 event in America in 1970 completely stunned both manufacturers and fans. When the competition was opened to 750cc machines of any type for the first time, it was Bob Hansen, the American parts manager for Honda, who suggested the Japanese company should enter. To his surprise, Honda sent four machines over from their factory to compete. Outwardly, to the untrained eye at least, the bikes were standard production CB750s. The four racers had in fact been subject to a comprehensive tune-up by the Honda Racing Service Centre.

The Honda factory had been reluctant to enter Daytona unless they could be sure of having more than a good chance of winning. The race was to be a four way battle for supremacy in the lucrative American motorcycle market between the Japanese Honda CB750s,

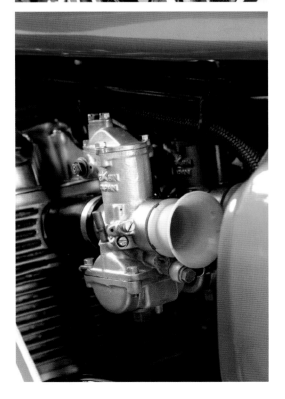

a British team of Triumph and BSA 750cc triples built specially for Daytona, the established American challenge of the Harley Davidson XR750s, and smaller capacity two-strokes from Suzuki and Kawasaki that presaged the beginning of the end for the four-strokes.

The four cylinder Honda CR750s, as they later became known, looked like they might have come from the works race shops of Gilera or MV. Whilst based very closely on the producion CB750s, many parts had been adapted or upgraded to ensure they would be competitive on the high-banked oval track and tight infield turns of the Daytona racetrack. Famously, Ralph Bryans, the No 1 rider in an impressive Honda team line-up including American Dick Mann, Bill Smith and Tommy Robb, crashed on the banking and his CR750 burned to a crisp with a ferocity that betrayed the expensive and weight-saving high magnesium and titanium content that was not found in the CB750s available to the public. In order to comply with the strict AMA homologation rules for the Daytona race, Honda was forced to make available race kits of all the special parts used in the CR750s, so that in theory at least, it was possible for customers to turn their CB750 into a bona fide race machine. This kit comprised of nearly 200 items, including high compression pistons, an entirely new head with altered valves, a higher lift camshaft, special con-rods, close ratio gears, uprated clutch and other trick engine parts. Almost all the cycle parts were upgraded; the large hand crafted aluminium fuel tank, four swept-back megaphone exhausts, twin front disc brakes, rear swing arm and twin leading-shoe rear drum brake. As a result, several frame alterations were necessary to accommodate new parts such as rear-set footpegs and the streamlined racing fairing. In following years, complete new frame kits were commissioned to improve handling from specialist race shops like Dresda.

In the early stages of the race, Mike Hailwoood and and Gary Nixon led on the British triples, but had to pull out due to engine problems. Mechanical issues hit the Honda team also, and Bryans' and Robb's CR750s were forced to drop out. It was Dick Mann who took the checkered flag, appropriately securing what was to prove a very valuable and significant victory for Honda on American soil, and ending the dominance of Britain and America in motorcycle showrooms around the world. The Japanese had arrived.

Rob North
Triumph Trident
750cc 1975 UK

Engine: 3 cyl.
Valves: Overhead valve
Capacity: 46cu / 750 cc
Power: Aprox. 80hp / 60kw

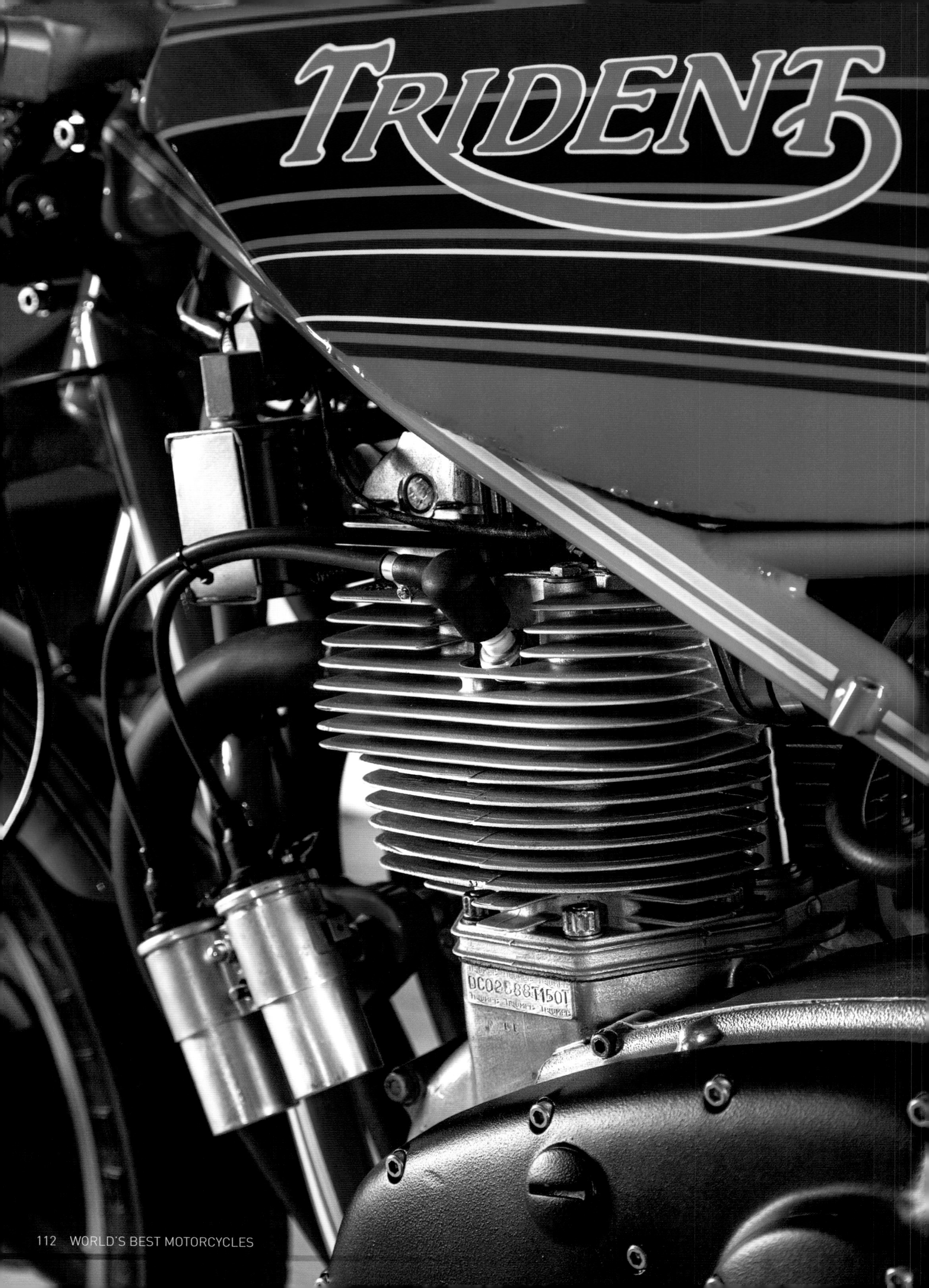
TRIDENT

Daytona 200. One of the greatest motorcycle races and, at the dawn of the 1970s, the scene of a desperate bid for glory and world markets by the fading British Motorcycle industry in the form of a three cylinder muscle bike produced jointly by Triumph and BSA as, respectively, the Trident and Rocket. This is the machine that was built in Britain to beat the mighty Harley Davidson XRTTs and the astonishing new Honda CR750 Fours from Japan, loosely based on the production CB750 and newly eligible to race at Daytona through the introduction of Formula 750 racing.

By the end of the 1960s the British 650 twin was well established in the key American market, winning races every weekend on dirt ovals all around the country and ridden to work during the week by everyone from farm hands to movie stars. But as broken crankshafts were beginning to prove, the traditional twin-cylinder engine layout was stretched to its tuning limits and beyond. Basing the new triple cylinder design on the old 500cc vertical twin, Triumph and its then parent company, BSA, pooled thinking in 1964 to add a third cylinder and each company produced their own version of a tough 750cc engine with a chunky, well supported crank with four main bearings that delivered something like 60 horsepower in standard form as the BSA Rocket 3 and Triumph Trident.

It wasn't just bragging rights that were at stake; critical American sales of the British 'Beezumphs' as they became known were threatened not only by Harleys but also a tide of modern exotica from the east; Hondas, Yamahas, Suzukis, with push-button starting, oil-tight reliability and attractive, high-quality finishes.

The Trident was a bike that right out of the showroom could challenge race-tuned Production 650cc Bonnevilles, with a top speed of around 130 mph (210 kmph). A special frame was commissioned from Rob North for the Daytona race teams to handle the power of the heavy unit-construction engine for the 1970 Daytona 200. Custom frame builders in Britain like Rob North, the Rickman brothers, Dave Degens of Dresda fame, Colin Seeley and others had long recognised that power was nothing without control, building sweet-handling after-market chassis kits that were used by racers keen to improve their chances racing home-tuned production machines. And if a customer wanted to build a bike like the one he saw Gene Romero, Gary Nixon, Don Castro or even Mike Hailwood, Paul Smart and Percy Tait riding at Daytona, he could order up a fancy frame kit from Rob North and reproduce a racer for the road in his own garage. Engine tuning was familiar and relatively straightforward, as all the tweaks learned on the old 500cc and 650cc twins had the same effect on the big 750. The finished article, built by an amateur with some rudimentary engineering skill and a decent set of spanners could

be very similar to the machine Gene Romero was timed on at over 165 mph on the banked oval track at Daytona.

The Rob North frame went through a number of detail changes during its development in racing in the early '70s, including dropping around 2 inches from the original so-called 'Highboy' design to the 'Lowboy' which as the name suggests had a lower centre of gravity and profile. Triples ran at Daytona on both wire-spoked and mag wheels, quickly moving from drum brakes on the early bikes to triple discs that were more effective in hauling the mass of the big triple to a halt.

The Daytona racing Triumphs were finished in vivid blue and white, the BSAs in flashy red and white, colours neatly appealing to both British and American fans. This example is in blue, appropriately for a Triumph-engined machine, with accurately period 70s graphics.

The first batch of the racers back in the 70s ran with a bank of three Amal GP carburetors but switched to 30mm Mk 1 Concentrics the following year which some considered as easier to set and balance. Standard production machines were fitted with four speed gearboxes but the racers were equipped with special five speed clusters from Quaife, which almost caused a problem with homologation. Although it was the Honda CR750 ridden by Dick Mann that won Daytona in 1970, the howling triples with their three-into-one megaphone exhausts caught the public's imagination and dominated racing for a brief but ear-shattering moment in in the early 70s. But there was another sound coming up the track, and even Doug Hele, who had done and given so much to keep Triumph out in front for so long, couldn't help but hear it; the spine-tingling scream of Japanese two-strokes like the Kawasaki H2 and Suzuki T500.

Some things, however, reassuringly stayed the same, like the pool of oil that invariably formed under the inexplicably vertically-split Triumph triples' crankcases. Big, brutal, with an outline that was drawn in countless schoolboys' exercise books and often literally built in a shed, the Rob North Triple was every inch the swansong of a once proud world-beating industry.

Harley-Davidson
XR1000 1983 *USA*

Engine:	V-twin
Valves:	Overhead valve
Capacity:	61cu / 996 cc
Power:	104hp / 77kw
Weight:	450lbs / 204kg
Top Speed:	150mph / 241kmh

Daytona was the scene for the inaugural race of the Battle of The Twins (BoTT) race series in 1981. The season was made up of eight rounds and with sales sluggish in the face of competition from multi-cylinder exotica from Europe and Asia, the Harley-Davidson management decided to make a concerted effort to use the 1000cc limit races as a marketing opportunity to try and rekindle enthusiasm for their traditional V twins. To do this, they needed a racer that was as close to the BoTT capacity as possible.

The Harley-Davidson XR1000 was based on the unit-construction 883 ohv XL sportster design that had been introduced way back in 1957. Released in small numbers, with only about 1,500 being made it was intended to be exactly what Harley enthusiasts had been demanding for years; a race-bred machine for the street, modeled on the all-conquering Harley-Davidson dirt-tracker, the XR750.

The XR750 had been launched in 1970 to pick up the racing reins from the flat-head KR introduced in 1952, which by the mid sixties was stoically, but not always successfully, holding off the mounting challenge of the British twins on dirt ovals around the country. In 1972, the XR750 was introduced, uprated by Pieter Zylstra from the old heavy iron heads and barrels to lightweight aluminium, and a legend was born. The beautifully streamlined orange and black tank and seat unit made the racing XR look like it was a blur of speed even when it was at a standstill, and with over 90 horsepower on tap, in the right hands it could drift into a corner and hurl itself up into the next straight quicker than all the competition.

The XR750 dominated flat-tracking in the 70's with the irrepressible AMA National Champion, Jay Springsteen, lifting title after title. AMF, the owner of the business, didn't hear, or chose to ignore, the calls by enthusiasts for a street-going version of the race bike, and it was not until Willie G and the Harley-Davidson management managed to buy back the company in 1981 that a road-going version of the racer was seriously considered. In the previous decade, racers like Cal Raybourne had shown what the XR750 was capable of when he diced so memorably with Ray Pickrell in the hard-fought Transatlantic Match Races of the early 70s, and the Battle of

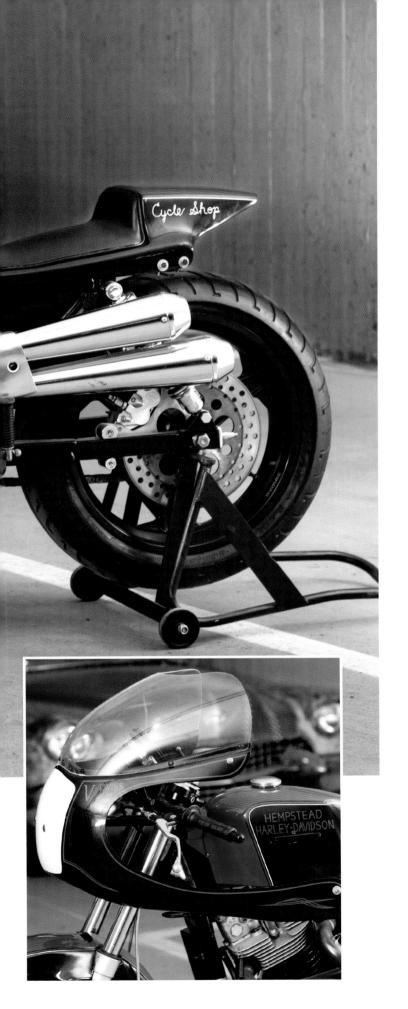

The Twins series provided another opportunity to remind customers of what Harley Davidson had once stood for.

The start of the BoTT season at Daytona in 1983 was chosen as both the moment for the company to officially re-enter road racing after a gap of around ten years and to launch the street XR1000.

Jay Springsteen won the 1983 race on an XR created in the Harley race shop by the maestro, Dick O'Brien, head honcho of the HD competition development. Dubbed 'Lucifer's Hammer', Springsteen's bike was, incredibly, to go on to win again in '84, '85 and '86. The street version of the XR1000 was less aggressive, but not by much, slamming out around 70bhp from its 998cc 45 degree oversquare V-twin engine and trick XLR aluminium heads with muscled-up cams. Fully factory race-kitted, the XR1000 was good for nearer 95 bhp. Twin Dell'Orto 36mm carbs with K&N filters were both set on the right hand side of the motor, while the matt black painted exhausts unusually both exited on the right, and at the front of the cylinders in order to assist cooling. There was little compromise for the street. Suspension was hard and unforgiving on the stock model, the twin discs were savage, and this example, campaigned on the track for several years by Rick Ranno, has been race prepared with tuned engine, added fairing, belly pan, rear-set pegs, and uprated Marzocchi front forks. The engine packs so much low-down torque from low revs, only four speeds were necessary. The big XR's acceleration was astonishing for road bike of the time and the biggest, perhaps the only real disappointment for customers was that it was finished in a dull-looking grey rather than an imitation of the orange and black Harley-Davidson racing livery. The XR1000's biggest drawback however, was its price; at around $7000 it simply couldn't attract enough buyers. In 1985, it rumbled off the catalogue list, although racing versions continued to battle it out against rival twins for years to come.

Hailwood, Graham, Ubbiali. Hartle, Surtees, Read, Agostini. Only the Champions of Champions rode the red and silver Gallarate 'fire engines' on the race tracks of Europe between the opening of the factory in 1946 to the late 1970s. Road-going MVs were available, but in limited numbers and at around three times the price of a Honda CB750 which had a better finish and reliable electrics. Following Count Agusta's death, and the rise to prominence on racetracks of Japanese two-strokes, production of both the racing and the road MVs wound down until production finally petered out in 1978. It was a slow decline for a once-great factory that had won every kind of honour on the track, and was arguably the most successful racing team in the history of motorcycle sport.

Many felt that the heritage should be allowed to rest in peace, that any attempt to resuscitate the brand would sully the hard-won reputation of the marque. It was not until the early 1990s that Claudio Castiglioni, the head of Cagiva, began to plot the return of MV Agusta with Massimo Tamburini, the obsessive genius of Bimota and Ducati 916 fame. Cagiva had secured the rights to use the MV Agusta name for a motorcycle and the F4 was developed in secret at the Cagiva Research Centre in Varese. From the start, Tamburini was determined that the new MV Agusta would be a fitting tribute to one of the greatest names in motorcycling and would blend the very best of motorcycling technology with superlative design in one the most advanced sports bikes of its time. The narrow four cylinder 749.8cc engine design with 73.8mm x 43.8mm bore and stroke benefitted from technological input by Ferrari, and featured an advanced radial 16 valve cylinder head and a racing-style six speed removable cassette gear cluster. The bodywork and styling by Tamburini made the F4 an instant classic that shares the indefinable style of the original MV Agusta racing machines, style that is wholly aligned with function.

The Oro, or 'Gold' edition of the F4 was limited to a numbered and plated run of just 300 units and differed from the Strada in a number of significant details. Many aluminium parts such as the wheels, swingarm

and engine contain high levels of magnesium for weight saving and were anodised gold to help prevent oxidisation. Carbon fibre was used extensively to further reduce weight and shave over 20lbs from the standard versions and the bodywork features quick release clips and fasteners, as it would be on a track machine. Suspension was class-leading with Showa forks that can be fully adjusted, as can the steering head angle, and Sachs and Ohlins rear shock assemblies. The exhaust was a work of art in itself, joining from four outlet pipes to two, then down into one, then back out to two and exiting under the seat unit once again as four and giving the F4 a unique sound.

Engine: 4-cyl transverse
Valves: DOHC 16 radial valve
Capacity: 46cu / 749 cc
Power: 130 bhp / 97kw
Weight: 400lbs /181kg

The F4's illustrious race lineage is very apparent and the F4 Serie d'Oro had adjustable footpegs, rear ride height and swing-arm settings, although rider ergonomics are uncompromising, from the minimal seat to the low setting of the clip-on handlebars, six-piston brakes and hard suspension. Despite its racing character the nimble-handling machine has impressive stability and faultless Weber-Marelli fuel injection even at low speeds around town. The MV Agusta is, however, without doubt at its finest when ridden hard, in the spirit of its ancestors, through twisting bends. Its greatest endorsement is perhaps that World Champion Giacomo Agostini personally pre-ordered his own F4 Serie d'Oro.

Vyrus 984 C3 2V 2007 *ITALY*

Engine:	Ducati V Twin 2 valve air-cooled
Capacity:	1000cc
Power:	90.5bhp / 67.5kw at 8,000rpm
Weight:	330lbs / 150kg
Top speed:	180mph / 290kmh

When the owner of Rimini-based Vyrus Motorcycles, Ascanio Rodorigo, and his team went to work on designing the Vyrus, he did so, in his own words, on 'a blank sheet of paper'. Rodorigo deliberately set out to challenge the perceived wisdom of motorcycle design and find new ways to approach the concepts of motorcycle construction.

The result is a meticulously detailed rolling sculpture in the finest traditions of the great designers, with modern echoes of past triumphs of visionary designers like Phil Irving and John Britten. The Vyrus is a motorcycle that shuns conventional wisdom in the

uncompromising pursuit of perfection. Like Vincent and Britten, Rodorigo and his team dispensed with a conventional frame and instead used the powerplant as the central stressed member, suspending from it the front and rear wheels, steering and suspension.

Ascanio Rodorigo worked at Bimota, the famous motorcycle frame-building firm, early in his career in the early 1980s, where he overlapped with Massimo Tamburini, who later went on to design those icons of motorcycle design, the Ducati 916 and MV Agusta F4. Where Tamburini clothed his masterpieces in drag-defying carbon fibre, Rodorigo and his team took the minimalist path, stripping the Vyrus back to the bone in a single-minded effort to cut weight down to MotoGP racing weight. Everything on the bike has been designed to minimise mass, from the stunningly crafted swingarm to individual bolts. The heart of the Vyrus 984 C3 machine is a Ducati 2 valve, aircooled V-twin engine with a capacity of nearly 1000cc giving 90.5hp. The Ducati engine forms the inflexible spine of the motorcycle, to which all other major components are attached.

The front end of the Vyrus is perhaps the most striking aspect of the innovative design. There are those that dismiss hub-centre steering as the wilful denial of the supremacy of the telescopic fork that has completely dominated motorcycle front suspension layout since the Second World War, with the notable exception of the Yamaha GTS1000. The small Vyrus workshop with its team of talented and specialist engineers from Bimota and Ducati had already produced the amazing and ground-breaking hub-centre steering Tesi 2D. Rodorigo wanted to push the boundaries

still further with the Vyrus 984 C3, convinced that hub-centre steering gives a massive handling advantage of eradicating dive and squat under braking or acceleration into and out of corners. This makes the lightweight Vyrus with its fearsome power-to-weight ratio feel consistently stable and secure when ridden hard even under normal, imperfect road conditions. On the track, it makes ultra-late braking and aggressive cornering on the Vyrus seem relaxed, despite the motorcycle's comparatively short wheelbase and radical chassis geometry.

Rodorigo and his team at Vyrus created a pared-down racer for the road in the 984 C3, giving exceptional care to the design and fabrication of every detail. The result is a limited edition, highly exclusive superbike.

Engine: Ducati V Twin 2 valve air-cooled
Capacity: 61cu / 1000cc
Power: 90.5bhp / 67.5kw at 8,000rpm
Weight: 330lbs / 150kg
Top speed: 180mph / 290kmh

sportsbike for the road, incredibly using the same boxer engine layout and technology that the German marque has championed very successfully both on and off the track for most of the last century. This model, conceived by BMW to contest the World Endurance Championship in 2007, boasts a four-valve double-overhead camshaft version of the historic boxer engine design that brings it screaming into the 21st century through its low-slung, all stainless-steel exhaust system.

The HP2 carries state-of the art racing-spec four piston monobloc Brembo radial-mounted brakes and the very pinnacle of fully-adjustable Ohlins suspension coupled with the famed BMW Telelever front end that is good enough to cope with a twenty-four hours thrash

around the Bol d'Or or a spin down the local high street. This gives the HP2 surprisingly advanced handling, despite the antique geometry of the transverse air-cooled cylinders jutting out from each side. Even so, without winding up the suspension settings, the carbon cam covers can ground on aggressive cornering, so were fitted at the factory with nylon sliders.

Weight has been kept to a minimum of just under 180kg through liberal use of carbon fibre for bodywork and even the rear subframe. The HP2 exemplifies refined, top quality German engineering and is the first production motorcycle from any manufacturer to be equipped as standard with 'Quickshifter' technology for race-bike clutchless gear changes up and down through the six-speed gearbox on the road. The HP2 is perfectly capable of dicing with pure-bred racing machinery on the track, knocking out 140hp from its high-revving twin cylinders. Japanese water-cooled four-cylinder racers may deliver more horsepower, but the overall combination of power, handling and weight make the HP2 a surprisingly competitive package.

Riding position is easily and quickly adjustable, as might be expected of a machine with a direct lineage to endurance racing. Sophisticated electrics are typically reliable and feature an on-board computer system for recording lap times, fuel consumption, revs and other vital stats from the Sunday morning blast.

Produced between 2008 and 2012, the HP2's heart, the new 4-valve design of the boxer engine was to continue, carried forward into the R1200GS. BMW has always believed in sticking with tradition, ever since the visionary young designer Max Friz set out his unconventional design for the BMW R47 in the 1920s. Friz's original flat-twin engine layout has remained the key identifying feature of progressively high-spec BMWs for succeeding model generations. Rejecting what he considered to be dirty and unreliable chain drive, Friz gave the R47 simple but reliable and tough shaft transmission, staying true to his Bauhaus-inspired concepts of clean, integral functionality. The HP2 may well be the ultimate incarnation of the great Friz design. But that has surely been prematurely assumed many times in the past.